LIFE STORIES

Hannah Hiles

NATIONAL
MEMORIAL
ARBORETUM

First published in 2010

National Memorial Arboretum
Croxall Road, Alrewas, Staffs DE13 7AR

Where our Nation remembers

Foreword

Two years ago, when I wrote the foreword to the current National Memorial Arboretum guidebook, I said 'In addition to the wide range of young trees on our 150 acre site you will find much, much more of interest. There are stories to tell behind every plot and monument, each of which tells a tale of heroism, of sadness, of a particular event or campaign or just of selfless devotion to duty.' It was, however, quickly pointed out to me that there was very little material actually to support this assertion, although we knew it to be very true.

Hannah Hiles' masterful case studies are a first stage in filling this void. Each one is carefully researched and sensitively written. The case studies are also already influencing our thinking about how we present the Arboretum to the public, in particular in the Remembrance Centre which forms a key part of the current NMA Appeal.

I know you will be greatly moved reading these stories in this magnificently produced and illustrated volume which I warmly commend to you.

Charlie Bagot Jewitt
CEO, National Memorial Arboretum
Part of The Royal British Legion family

Preface

When I first visited the National Memorial Arboretum in July 2007, the site was just drying out from unseasonal and particularly intense rain storms and the stunning Armed Forces Memorial was still a work in progress.

I was at the Arboretum to interview chief executive Charlie Bagot Jewitt for a magazine article, and as he showed me around the growing site, his enthusiasm and passion proved infectious. I was captivated by the memorials, by what they stood for and by what this restored gravel quarry, generously gifted by Lafarge, was becoming.

And the more I thought about it, the more I wanted to know. Who were the people whose names were being painstakingly inscribed on the Armed Forces Memorial? Who was represented by the blindfolded young man at Shot At Dawn? The historical answers could be found in the guidebook but the human stories, the stories of lost loved ones and long-cherished memories, had yet to be told.

It has been an honour to work on this collection of biographical stories from behind the memorials. I'm in awe at the irrepressible positivity of Elaine Betts, Janet Booth's fight for justice, Frank Shorter's good humour under fire, Carl Grundy's tireless fundraising in his twin brother's name and the strength that came out of Jenny Green's sorrow. It is impossible not to be moved and inspired by the people who are commemorated at the Arboretum and by the people they left behind.

Having scratched the surface I will never look at these memorials in the same way again. I now understand more fully just what an important place this is. It is a place where every detail has a meaning and a place where there is always something new to discover. And it is a place which means something different to every person.

The trees of the National Memorial Arboretum form a living tribute to those who have gone before us and while we remember them, they are never far away.

Hannah Hiles

The break of a new dawn

Uncovering a family secret lead to a 14-year fight to clear a grandfather's name

Janet Booth grew up, like so many others, knowing little more about her grandfather besides the fact that he had been killed in World War One.

A generation had been all but wiped out and her mother and grandmother never did anything to suggest the circumstances might have been unusual.

It was only when Janet was planning a family holiday to France in the mid 1980s that she learned what had happened.

"I had been tracing my family tree and as we were going to France I thought I would look up Harry's grave. When I asked where he was buried there was a look between my mum and grandmother. My grandmother said: 'Well, he was shot for cowardice. He doesn't have a grave.' That was the first I had heard of it. I was shocked and thought it was a dreadful thing to have happened. It took time to sink in that he had been executed."

The sense of shame surrounding the secret was so strong that Janet's mother Gertrude Harris had only learned the truth about her father at the age of 40 after a family gathering. Her aunt, who had moved abroad after the war without knowing the full details of her brother's death, asked: "What's all this I hear about Harry?" The subject was quickly changed but Gertrude later tackled her mother, also named Gertrude.

Private Harry Farr of the 1st Battalion West Yorkshire Regiment was just 25 years old when he died.

Having already served as a regular soldier, Harry went out to France with the British Expeditionary Force in November 1914. He saw action at the battle of Neuve Chappelle in March 1915, where British troops suffered heavy losses, and fought at Aubers Ridge in May. Soon afterwards, he was diagnosed with shell shock and spent five months in hospital in France. He rejoined his battalion in October 1915, but spent a couple of weeks in hospital again the following year.

In September 1916 he was going up to the front with the ration party when he asked if he could fall out and went back to the dressing station. The medical officer said that as he did not have any visible injuries he had to go back but Harry just could not do it. For refusing orders he was put on a charge and court martialled. His court martial was held a month later. It lasted just 20 minutes.

The court martial papers show that he defended himself. He said: "On the sergeant-major's return I reported to him and said I was sick and could not stand it. He then said: 'You are a f****** coward and you will go to the trenches. I give f*** all for my life and I give f*** all for yours and I'll get you f****** well shot'.

"The Sgt. Maj. then told L. Cp. Form to fall out two men and take me up to the Trenches. They commenced to shove me. I told them not to as I was sick enough as it was. The sergeant-major then grabbed my rifle and said: 'I'll blow your f****** brains out if you don't go'. I then called out for an officer but there were none there. I was then tripped up and commenced to struggle. After this I do not know what happened until I found myself back in the 1st Line Transport under a guard. If the escort had not started to shove me about I would have gone up to the Trenches: it was on account of their doing this that I commenced to struggle."

When asked why he had not reported sick before the alleged offence he replied that when away from the sound of the gunfire he felt better.

A regimental captain said of Harry in a report: "I cannot say what has destroyed this man's nerves, but he has proved himself on many occasions incapable of keeping his head in action and likely to cause a panic. Apart from his behaviour under fire, his conduct and character are very good."

Despite this, the Lieutenant General said: "The charge of 'cowardice' seems to be clearly proved and the Sergeant Major's opinion of the man is definitely bad to say the least of it. The GOC 6th Div. informs me that the men know the man is no good. I therefore recommend that the sentence be carried out."

And so it was. Harry Farr was executed by shooting at 6am on October 18, 1916, at Carnoy. He refused a blindfold. "Maybe he felt he had seen hell and knew what it looked like," says Janet.

"What must his frame of mind have been like?"

Harry's widow Gertrude received an official letter telling her that he had been shot for showing cowardice. She kept the news to herself before finally admitting it to her parents and in-laws. Harry's father was a military man and was so ashamed that he would not allow family members to mention his name in front of him, but on Remembrance Day Harry's brothers would raise a glass to him in the pub.

"Afterwards my grandmother was left virtually destitute," says Janet. "Her pension was stopped and, at 21 years of age with a three-year-old daughter to support, she became homeless before finding a job as a kitchen maid.

"My grandmother was a tiny little woman but very strong. She was like that because of what she went through. There were no benefits or counselling; you just had to keep a stiff upper lip and get on with it."

And it was thanks to Janet's grandmother that the 14-year campaign to get a pardon for Harry took off.

In 1992 she happened to see a television interview with Andrew McKinlay, Labour MP for Thurrock, who said he was going to try to secure pardons for the 306 men executed following WW1 court martials. She called her granddaughter in great excitement and Janet decided to write to the MP explaining Harry's case.

Andrew McKinlay introduced Janet to military historian Julian Putkowski, who worked hard to obtain official papers and information relating to the case, although unfortunately Harry's medical records were lost during WW2.

"I wanted to do it for my grandmother," says Janet. "She always believed that Harry was suffering from shell shock and was not a coward. The last correspondence she had from him was a field card sent during his time in hospital in 1915 – it was written by a nurse because Harry couldn't hold a pen as his hand shook so much.

"Once we got his court martial papers we could really see what had happened. Before that we couldn't prove what he had or hadn't done because there was no access to the records until the government released the papers."

The family launched a campaign to take the Ministry of Defence to court on Harry's behalf. At the same time a group called the Shot At Dawn Campaign was fighting to clear the names of all 306 men.

Andrew McKinlay and Julian Putkowski visited Janet's grandmother in early 1993 and she poured her heart out and told them everything. She passed away in August that year, having got it all off her chest. Julian recorded her story and it was used in a BBC Radio 4 documentary called With Regrets. A copy is also held at the Imperial War Museum.

The Shot At Dawn campaign gathered pace and in 1999 the family was allowed to attend a service in London alongside war widows the day before Remembrance Day. "The media descended on my mother and she told them all about how it felt to find out about her father. She was only one when he went to France so she doesn't remember him at all."

After several trips to the High Court, meetings with senior ministers, a volume of paperwork and numerous setbacks ("John Major opposed a pardon, saying that you can't rewrite history."), the family finally got the news they wanted to hear in August 2006, that Harry Farr had received a conditional pardon. The other men received conditional pardons in October of that year.

"At first when I got the call I just wrote the message down on a piece of paper," says Janet. "It didn't really sink in. Then the phone started ringing. I couldn't get through to my mum because her phone was so busy; she didn't sleep that night. Andrew McKinlay called me from Australia to see if it was really true and at 6am Sky News were outside the house waiting to interview me. It had taken 14 years to secure this pardon and I couldn't believe it.

"We have never been interested in compensation – we just wanted to clear his name and remove the stigma. You can only go so far and a conditional pardon is good enough for us. Every one of those 306 men was someone's son, someone's dad. They wanted to fight for king and country but didn't know what they were going out to."

Harry's name is on the Thiepval Memorial to the Missing monument at The Somme, commemorating soldiers without graves, and is also named at the Shot At Dawn memorial at the National Memorial Arboretum. Janet's mother Gertrude Harris helped to unveil the monument in 2001, along with John Hipkin, the founder of the Shot At Dawn Campaign.

"When the memorial at the NMA was first unveiled it was one of the only places we could go to pay our respects to our loved ones," says Janet. "It was thought that these men did not deserve graves so at least we could go to the Shot At Dawn memorial and think about him there and reflect on what had happened. It's just such a peaceful place."

Despite living with the manner of her husband's death throughout her life, Janet's grandmother, who later re-married, always remembered Harry as the handsome young man in his early twenties who she had met when she was just 16.

"She said he was a handsome, gentle man with curly hair and deep grey eyes, not green like it said on his Army papers," says Janet. "She was in service when she started going out with him. He would stand at the end of the road and whistle, and she would pretend to the mistress of the house that she was going out to post a letter.

"She always remembered him as a 23-year-old going out to France. She still loved him as he was then – he never got old to her. She always preserved his memory and she would be proud to know he has been pardoned."

• • •

Breath of Life

*Elaine remembers the donor who gave
her a new lease of life with a tree at the
National Memorial Arboretum*

This tree is in memory of
my lung donor without whom
I would never have experienced
the pleasures of breathing;
she will be forever in my
thoughts
Elaine Betts

Elaine Betts has always lived life to the full despite suffering from a serious illness, but when her health deteriorated dramatically she relied on a lung donor to save her life.

And, a year after the successful transplant operation, she decided to pay tribute to this unknown woman with a tree and plaque at the National Memorial Arboretum.

Born in 1970, Elaine was diagnosed with genetic disease cystic fibrosis at the age of three. No one expected her to reach her seventh birthday but her family – mum Annie, dad Frank and older brother Neil – encouraged her to lead a normal life.

Elaine needed physiotherapy first thing in the morning and last thing at night, but never had a day off school, despite her teachers being nervous about having a pupil who carried so much medication with her.

"My mum fought my corner and made sure I was treated like every other child," says Elaine, who comes from Norton Canes in Staffordshire.

As a six-year-old Elaine took up ballroom, disco and Latin American dancing and went on to gain all her dance medals before she stopped at 18 when she, as she puts it, "discovered night clubs and alcohol". She was also a keen horse rider and a Brownie and Guide "Everyone wanted to share my tent on camps," she says, "because I was the only one whose tent had a built-in groundsheet."

Going to friends' birthday parties posed a challenge as at that time, people with cystic fibrosis were not allowed to eat fatty foods. Elaine became known as the "jam sandwich girl" because she took them to parties and never touched the cakes, chocolate and ice cream that the other guests enjoyed. But never having tried these forbidden foods, Elaine didn't mind going without and the other children never made an issue of it.

Staff at the Manor Hospital in Walsall taught her to know what she wanted in terms of her treatment and how to stand up for herself. "The doctors all regret it now," laughs Elaine.

When she hit high school her health began to deteriorate and in her early teens she had to start using nebulisers and intravenous drugs. Despite this, she says she continued to "just get on with things."

"I never wanted to rebel and I always took it quite seriously. I had an old head on my shoulders when it came to my body. I was very good at planning my days to get everything in and I was quite strict with myself.

"I've always been a positive person and never let it get to me. I try to get around things and look for alternatives rather than letting anything stop me."

By 1986 the food rules had changed for people with cystic fibrosis and Elaine was encouraged to eat as much fat as possible. From being the "jam sandwich girl" she became the "Jaffa Cake girl" as she ate so many every day.

"I came to loathe this new diet within the first week," she says. "What made it even more traumatic was the fact that I never appeared to gain any weight despite all the efforts of the dieticians."

Elaine left school at 16 and faced what she sees as one of the major challenges of her life – getting a job in the days before the Disability Discrimination Act and juggling hospital appointments with full-time work.

She started a Youth Training Scheme with British Coal, going to college on day release, but she had only been there a month when she became diabetic, a condition which can be linked to cystic fibrosis. "I wasn't expecting this at all," says Elaine. "The hospital wanted to keep me in to show me how to inject myself, but I said 'just give me the needles and let me do it'."

Despite this setback, Elaine was offered a permanent position with British Coal within three months of starting the scheme and she stayed with them for 13 years. "They introduced me to studying and I have never stopped," she says. She now works for Walsall Council and is about to complete a postgraduate level qualification in the Chartered Institute of Personnel and Development Professional Development Scheme.

In 1989 her medical care was transferred to a specialist CF unit at Heartlands Hospital in Birmingham – "they had

the difficult job of keeping me alive while I worked full-time and refused to take things easy" – and in 1993 she had her first transplant assessment at Wythenshawe Hospital in Manchester. The doctors agreed with Elaine that she was too well for a double lung transplant at this time, but in 1995 she was placed on the active transplant list.

After eight months her health stabilised and she was "frozen" on the list, which meant they would no longer look for a donor but would monitor her health – and as soon as it began to deteriorate she would go back on the active list.

In 2000 Elaine began to require more frequent IV drugs and in typical style, continued to live her life as normal, taking her drugs into work and even to the gym.

She had another transplant assessment in July 2002, and went back on the active transplant list on November 19, the week before she accepted a new job offer. Nonetheless she started her new job in January 2003.

Her health began to deteriorate rapidly and in November 2003 Elaine made the difficult decision to stop working and studying. "I decided to put my organisational skills to good use by organising the final part of my life so I went and paid for my funeral," she says. "After all there is no point wasting the skills you have!"

But ill health did not hold Elaine back for long and in January 2004 she got another full-time job, which she started in June that year. Her new employer was supportive of her impending death or transplant and Elaine continued to take her IV drugs into work and retained her reputation for taking Jaffa Cakes everywhere. "The dieters in the office used to really envy me and I used to wave the food in front of them," she laughs.

By September 2004 she had to admit defeat and accept that she needed oxygen, much to the relief of her medical team, although she continued to work full-time and refused to use a wheelchair, despite having only a few weeks a year without a chest infection. She studied after work for a diploma in Training and Development, sat four exams and ended up in hospital the following day with kidney failure, more worried about her exam results than her health. She passed, of course.

But her health had taken a serious knock and she began to decline quickly. In March and April 2006 it became clear that she had very little time left when her lungs began to bleed. Although the doctors managed to stop the bleeding Elaine knew that it could have killed her at any time, and she decided to talk to her loved ones about her final days. "It was very traumatic for everyone but I'm always a realist," she says.

She had carried a pager for almost four years before the call came that a donor had been found on June 29, 2006, the day before a friend's wedding.

"I had said to my friend that I had a feeling I would not make it to her wedding," says Elaine. "I didn't even buy a dress until the last minute because I was so sure I would not be there. I had taken the day before the wedding off work to get ready and I was just about to put diamantes on my nails when I got the call.

"I never thought I would actually get the call although I always hoped I would. It's strange but I didn't panic I just felt relieved that at last my pain and suffering would be over one way or another.

"My parents and I just dropped everything – my suitcase had been packed for four years – and set off for the hospital in Manchester. I texted all my friends to say I had got the call and that I would see them later, although I didn't know if I would."

And so, when Elaine was wheeled into the operating theatre at 2am on June 30, she says she didn't look like the usual sick transplant patient – she was glowing from her beauty treatments and fake tan, with perfectly styled hair.

The first thing she saw when she opened her eyes after her double lung transplant was her mum, dad and brother. "I was so happy to get the chance to see them again and squeeze their hands," she says. "I remember thinking, if I don't make it through to the next stage at least I got the chance to open my eyes and see a different world."

Elaine spent five weeks in hospital and faced unexpected challenges in her recovery. "My first words when I came off the ventilator were 'I never knew breathing was so easy'. They didn't prepare me for coming off all the things that were keeping me alive. They literally took off my mask and I began to panic, then I just started breathing. It was a very strange sensation – I never realised that people didn't have to try to breathe."

At just 4'10" tall, Elaine had also been on the child transplant list, but in the end it was an adult donor that gave her a new lease of life. All she knows about her donor is that she was a 39-year-old Irish woman who had had a blood clot and died of a haemorrhage. Every year she writes a letter to her donor's family which gets passed on through the transplant team, telling them what she has been able to do thanks to their kindness.

Intriguingly, Elaine believes that her donor has given her more than just a new pair of lungs. "I am certain that I have taken on some of her traits," she says. "I was never creative before my transplant but during my recovery period I took up card making and I love it. I would never have had the patience to do this before but now I find it very relaxing.

"I was also always extremely punctual and used to get annoyed when my friends were even one minute late; now the tables have turned and I am never on time. And my taste in food has changed completely. I didn't used to like sauces and spices and preferred a plain diet, but now that bores me and I love spicy food. I didn't have much of an appetite before the operation and never knew food could be a pleasure. My donor has a lot to answer for!"

While Elaine takes more tablets now than before her operation – 15 different drugs each day, made up of 43 tablets and four injections – she no longer needs intravenous drugs and has not stayed in hospital overnight since 2006.

Eleven months after her transplant, Elaine took part in the BUPA Great Manchester 10km run to raise money for the Wythenshawe Transplant Fund New Start Charity, completing the course in one hour 51 minutes and 20 seconds, coming

20,994th out of 28,000 people. It took her three months to recover, but nonetheless she has since taken part in another 10km race.

To celebrate the first anniversary of her transplant Elaine planted an oak tree at the National Memorial Arboretum. She designed the memorial plaque herself – a pair of lungs containing two shamrocks – which reads: "This tree is in memory of my lung donor, without whom I would never have experienced the pleasures of breathing. She will be forever in my thoughts. Elaine Betts."

Elaine and her family visit the tree by the river regularly and plan to enjoy a cake in the shape of a clown there every year on the anniversary to commemorate the transplant.

"I love the Arboretum," says Elaine. "Although the memorials remember people who are no longer with us, there is nothing sad about it. It is such a beautiful and calm place."

Elaine kept a diary throughout her transplant journey to remind her what she went through. "It's what's made me who I am," she says. "Nobody knows how long I have left. It could be tomorrow, it could be 10 years. They never know how your body will react. Each time I get a cold it knocks my lung function. But if it comes tomorrow, I know I have had a great three years. Transplants really do change people's lives – I thought my life was fun before, but now it is beyond words."

• • •

Brothers in Arms

Carl Grundy honours his late twin brother by fundraising for the NMA

In the unlikely event that Carl Grundy ever forgot the year in which his twin brother was killed, he could just count the poppies surrounding the black-framed photograph on his wall.

Carl, a Sergeant in the Adjutant General's Corps, has kept every Armistice Day poppy he has worn since Andrew died in a bomb attack in Northern Ireland on May 1, 1992 at just 22 years old.

Andrew's name is listed on the Armed Forces Memorial ("the eighth name from the top, on panel 207," says Carl) and the family visit regularly to place a poppy wreath at the wall and a cross by his tree at the Arboretum's Ulster Grove.

Although not identical, the twins were always very close and shared a special bond. Andrew could feel Carl's pain "I once knelt on a glass bottle top and cut myself," says Carl, "and Andrew ran into the house screaming, even though there was nothing wrong with him.

"On another occasion he dared me to touch the fire in our house and when I suffered severe burns, he could feel it when I was having the skin grafts. I'll always carry my burn scars as another reminder of him."

For youngsters growing up in Ferryhill, south of Durham, joining the army was seen as one of the only options. Carl, whose AGC role covers human resources administration, joined the Army in 1986, straight from school at the age of 16-and-a-half. Serving in the armed forces was something of a family tradition. His father was in the navy and out of the six brothers including Carl, five have served in the army.

Although events in the Falklands were a recent memory, the young soldiers didn't think too much about the prospect of going to war.

"There was just no work available," says Carl, "and I needed a job. I just took every day as it came. It was quite a shock to the system – speak when you're spoken to, move when you're told to move."

Andrew, the younger of the twins, followed him into the army several years later. He was on his first deployment with the 2nd

Battalion Royal Regiment of Fusiliers when he was killed in the attack described as "one of the most sophisticated bomb attacks by the IRA throughout the conflict" at a permanent vehicle checkpoint near Killeen in County Armagh.

The checkpoint, Romeo One Five, was protected on three sides by armoured blast walls facing the main Belfast to Dublin road, with a railway line behind it. Members of the IRA loaded a stolen van with 1,000kg (2,200 lb) of Semtex and equipped it with wheels adapted to run on railway tracks. The van was lifted onto the tracks using a stolen JCB and driven to the top of a hill north of the checkpoint. At around 2am they put the van into gear and directed it towards the checkpoint, with 1,800 metres of command wire attached to a triggering device spooling from the back.

Andrew had just come on duty when he heard a warning over the radio from another checkpoint saying there was a car driving down the railway line. Looking out of his sangar he spotted the danger and alerted his fellow soldiers who were able to take shelter.

When the bomb detonated it blew the sentry box off its foundations and Andrew was killed by the blast. The other soldiers escaped with cuts and bruises.

Andrew had had a sense of foreboding about his deployment. "He had predicted he was going to get killed", says Carl, "but he was still happy to go out there. It is a soldier's job to protect the nation.

"I was at home when I heard the news. My younger brother called me and said Andrew had been killed. I realised later that my son Michael, who was just two months at the time, woke up at the exact time the device exploded, screamed, and went back to sleep. The Commanding Officer provided me with a car and I went straight to my parents."

The family were hit hard by their loss – especially as Carl had lost another brother in a car crash just eight months earlier – and the damage is still raw.

Despite his loss Carl's commitment to the armed forces never wavered and his military career has taken him around the world,

often in peacekeeping roles in places such as Kosovo, Bosnia and Northern Ireland.

He volunteered to go to Iraq in 2003, having never been deployed to a war zone, and served three tours of six months each. To his surprise he found the experience boring. "I was initially with the field hospital but when that got taken over by the Territorial Army I went back to the Transport regiment that I was detached from. I was never on the front line.

"At the end of the day I was deployed to a war zone but I was never in any danger. We used to drive round the villages and deliver food and water. It was interesting to see their culture and way of life. It was completely different from what we were used to and sometimes hard to watch."

Sadly Andrew's is the not the only familiar name on the Armed Forces Memorial and Carl has had to cope with losing friends and colleagues in Iraq.

"I have no regrets whatsoever about choosing this career," he says, "and no two days are the same. The best thing about it is the camaraderie – someone has always got your back – but the worst thing is seeing your friends getting killed. When I was in Iraq for the last time an officer and another couple of guys were killed. It was terrible, there was so much grief."

For Carl, the National Memorial Arboretum and the Armed Forces Memorial are vital in helping the nation recognise the sacrifices made by fallen service men and women.

He got involved with the Arboretum after he was invited to attend a tree planting ceremony organised by the Royal Regiment of Fusiliers in 2003 while serving in Iraq. This was the dedication of trees in the Ulster Grove for all those who lost their lives in Northern Ireland.

Since that first visit Carl has become a familiar face to the staff at the Arboretum and has visited on numerous occasions with his family. He was invited to the first Armistice Day ceremony at the Armed Forces Memorial in 2007 to represent young veterans and is a keen fundraiser for the NMA and AFM. In 2007 he completed a 150-mile cycle ride in 12-and-a-half

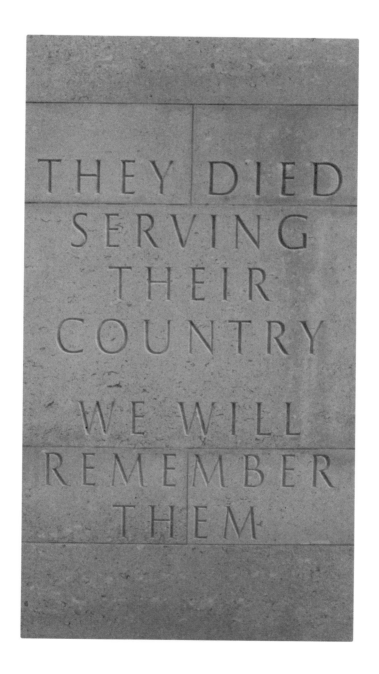

hours alongside 17 colleagues from the Adjutant General's Corps, raising almost £4,000, while in 2009 he spent 15 days in the saddle cycling from John O'Groats to Lands End on another fundraising mission. He has also been closely involved in the restoration of the Adjutant General's Corps monument, which was completed in September 2009.

"The Arboretum to me is a place where I can visit and just let the world pass me by as I tour the grounds without a care in the world and reflect on what sacrifices people, including Andrew, have made," he says.

"It is not only somewhere families can go and see the names of their loved ones and feel they are there, but other members of the public can also see all those names and begin to understand what these people have done for them.

"The Arboretum is not only about the sacrifices that have been made; that is what the Armed Forces Memorial and the numerous war memorials around the country are for. The Arboretum is about the trees – the memory of loved ones who have made the ultimate sacrifice lives on as the tree grows to provide a lasting memorial.

"The National Memorial Arboretum and the Armed Forces Memorial are places for remembrance and reflection on the past, present and future of our nation. I went up to the Armed Forces Memorial the day before it officially opened to present the cheques from the first cycle ride and was shown Andrew's name. I could only stand there for a couple of minutes because it was so moving. It is difficult to put into words how proud I feel when I see his name there."

• • •

Sunshine After The Rain

War widow Jenny Green has used her experience of personal tragedy to help hundreds of families cope

Jenny Green thought she knew what it was like to lose your husband until it happened to her. As the wife of a dedicated RAF man, she had already comforted many widowed friends when she found herself in their position.

Jenny and Bill met at Oxford University towards the end of their first year. They got engaged at the beginning of their third year and married in Oxford's Christ Church Cathedral as soon as they finished their exams. "In one respect my entire adult life was with Bill," says Jenny, who was born in India and brought up in Africa as her father was in the Colonial Service.

In Bill's first year at Oxford he was commissioned in the RAF. "He was passionate about flying fast jets – he would have liked to have been a racing driver, if he could have afforded it. Although I knew little about the RAF I realised that life with Bill would be nomadic and so I decided to do a post-graduate teaching qualification" says Jenny.

Where possible Jenny took teaching posts wherever Bill was based. The couple had a son and a daughter and spent time in Germany and the USA. But the family was based at RAF Marham in Norfolk when their lives changed forever.

Bill was essentially "a Harrier man", but was pleased to have been asked to command a Tornado squadron. He was promoted to Group Captain and was going to be the Tornado detachment commander in the first Gulf War. They were about to deploy to the Gulf, when he said that he had to go out and fly a training mission.

Bill and his fellow crew member were lost over the North Sea on the night of Thursday, August 16, 1990. Their bodies were never recovered.

"Having been part of the 'Harrier family', we had lost quite a few friends in the early days of the Harrier," says Jenny. "I had several friends who had been widowed and I thought I understood what it was like to lose your husband, but that night I found I had no idea. My whole world changed in a moment."

Jenny's friends descended on her to give support, but she soon realised that the widow of the other man lost in the crash did not have this network of people who understood what she was going through.

"I realised what a difference that made," she says. "Over the next week or so there were all sorts of things that were causing anxiety. I couldn't believe that the problems I faced were the same problems that people widowed 20 years earlier had had, and realised that the RAF must not have known what these problems were. There was no mechanism for any feedback.

"People felt they were 'excommunicated' from the service. It felt as though it was all mixed up, determining what pension you received was a complete muddle. I was even told I wasn't a war widow as my husband never reached the war. There appeared to be no coordinated system. At that time if you didn't know someone who had been through it and knew what to do it could be very difficult."

Jenny got a group of widows together with the aim of trying to make things better for the next generation of widows, and following that meeting they were asked to form an official organisation. The RAF Widows' Association was born, The Association gained charitable status in 1994 and has worked closely with the RAF to improve the system for all widows and their families, and helped both the army widows and navy widows form similar organisations. The RAF Widows' Association is officially recognised by the Ministry of Defence. Jenny was awarded the OBE in 2000 for her role.

Jenny found she enjoyed campaigning and was a committee member and leading campaigner for the War Widows' Association from 1995 to 2008, and also chair of the War Widows' Association from 2005 to 2008.

"The War Widows' Association is a pressure group and there were real issues we were fighting for. One of our successes was getting a pension for life in 2000. Previously a war widow lost the pension if she remarried or cohabited. I enjoyed championing the cause and making a difference.

"I was 42 when Bill died and I was left without my rudder. Through being a service wife I didn't have a career I had

committed to. I had been teaching when I could, but there had not been the opportunity to develop a career.

"After I lost Bill, my mother said to me: 'Look, you can't let this ruin the rest of your life. You can weep for the rest of your life, but it won't change it. There are some things you just can't do anything about and this is one of them, but you can still make a good life for yourself and your children.

"I had to make something good come out of Bill's death. He was bright, he was able; his career would have taken him far. It was such a waste of a life. In my heart of hearts the work that I have done since he died is to make something good from something senseless; it is my living memorial to my husband."

Jenny's influence extends beyond the realm of helping war widows come to terms with their bereavement. Among other high profile positions, she is a former chair of United Lincolnshire Hospitals NHS Trust and a trustee of the charity Combat Stress, which specialises in the care of British veterans who have been traumatised by harrowing experiences during their Service career, and for many years she has been on the Council of the Forces Pension Society.

Working with Cruse Bereavement Care as the project manager for their Armed Forces Project, she has tried to ensure that Cruse offers appropriate bereavement support to all who have been touched by a death in the Armed Forces. She has produced web-based information, training course material and a DVD of personal case stories so that all 5,000 Cruse volunteers and others in the community, who come in contact with bereaved service families, can better understand the emotions and feelings of those who have lost someone in the forces, and how a death in service can complicate the grieving process.

"Having been involved in helping improve things for widows I have become aware of the parents, brothers and sisters left behind and the lack of appropriate support for them, and I want to do something to help them too," she says. "A military death raises some complex issues that can affect the grieving process and they need support. They need to feel that they matter to

the forces, to have something to help make sense of their loss, and a recognition that they have an ongoing connection with the forces if they want it."

The Armed Forces Memorial at the National Memorial Arboretum is particularly close to Jenny's heart and she is a trustee of the memorial appeal.

"I know too many names on the Armed Forces Memorial, far too many," she says. "I remember standing there at the dedication; I suddenly turned and there was the name of a man whose wife I had had to break the bad news to in 1971.

"The names on the wall are all real people who have been part of my life and other people's lives. Each name represents a life lost and means something, not just to one person or one family, but to many, many people both now and in the future. "Like other families my children and I don't need a memorial to remember my husband, but it is important that my children will be able to take their children and show them their grandfather's name, especially as we have no grave to visit.

"The Armed Forces Memorial is a stunning and fitting tribute to all who have lost their lives in the services. The inscription on the obelisk says it all: 'in memory of those who died serving their country'."

• • •

The Unsung Hero

*As a stretcher jeep driver during the
Korean War Frank Shorter saved countless
wounded from death on the minefields*

Frank Shorter doesn't see himself as a hero, but in his role as a stretcher jeep driver during the Korean War he saved countless wounded men from death on minefields and brought back other comrades who had not been so fortunate.

A regular soldier from his 17th birthday in 1946, Frank had already served in Egypt, Palestine, the Middle East and Austria by the time he was sent to Korea with the Royal Leicestershire Regiment in July 1951.

Now Frank is one of more than 100 volunteers who give up their time and energy to work at the National Memorial Arboretum every week, and it's not unusual to hear a cry of "that ginger-haired so and so is still alive!" when he is spotted by a fellow veteran visiting the NMA.

Frank came from a military background. His four brothers, father and grandfathers were all in the army, and he felt it was expected of him to join up too.

By the age of 18 he was in Suez, Egypt, guarding German prisoners of war ("Rommel's merry men" he says,) before being transferred to Palestine and Jerusalem, where Jewish refugees were flooding into the area from the concentration camps in Europe. He then spent three years in the desert in the Middle East, where the heat was so oppressive that the day's work had to be finished by 9am.

After several months in Austria, Frank returned to his home in Birmingham to await demob in 1951 – but soon found himself called on to do an extra two years' service in Korea.

The troops lived in holes dug into trenches in freezing conditions. They couldn't wash and had to sleep with their clothes and boots on for fear of getting frostbite. The young soldier saw plenty of sights which stay with him to this day.

"Only a jeep could get up to the front line," says Frank. "I was known as a scrounger and I used to take coffee up with me for the men at the front. One day I was up there when all of a sudden the Sergeant Major shouted 'stand to!'.

"For some reason the mist lifted and we saw what looked like a great big brown blanket before us. It was 10,000 Chinese lying in wait for us. It was one of the most horrific sights I had seen. "The men at the back didn't have weapons; they were waiting for the men in front to get killed so they could use theirs. We managed to keep them back, but there was a big cost. We lost a lot of men that day."

Frank's role as a stretcher jeep driver took him into the minefields three or four times a day to pick up wounded and dead comrades. On one occasion a landmine exploded, destroying his jeep and throwing Frank and his four wounded passengers into the air. Frank carried one of the men back to base on his shoulders, not realising until he reached safety that he was injured himself, with shrapnel embedded in his head and arm.

"Someone once said 'you must have some guts' but it wasn't guts, it was just discipline," he says. "I was just doing what I was told to do. I don't think I was a brave man; people relied on me and I just did what I had to do. In our day, with the Second World War not long finished, there was discipline in the home as well as in the army. If you signed on to do five or seven years, you signed on to become a trained killer. I always said if there is a bullet with your name on it, you will get it, and if not, there was no point worrying."

This positive attitude won Frank many friends across the army who remember him to this day. In addition to the Royal Leicestershire Regiment, he also served with the Royal Lincolnshire Regiment, the Royal Warwickshire Regiment, the Coldstream Guards and the Sherwood Foresters during his military career, as well as working for the Ministry of Defence, the Prison Service and the Corps of Commissionaires once he left the army.

He first visited the Arboretum to take part in a military parade in 2005 and enquired that very day about voluntary work.

Now he is a well-known face at the Arboretum, particularly to visitors who are unable to walk around the 150-acre site. Frank is in charge of issuing wheelchairs and mobility scooters, and also drives visitors around in golf buggies.

But it isn't only his helpful nature which led him to be nominated for an Outstanding Contribution Award from the

Arboretum. His wide-ranging military knowledge and extensive memory for his former comrades have brought about some moving and astonishing experiences.

"Not long ago, an elderly woman arrived at the reception desk with a man in his fifties and two children," says Frank. "She had come to find the memorial to her brother, and as soon as I heard the name, I said 'the fitness fanatic!'. She asked me how I knew him, and I told her that I was the man who carried her brother off the field after he had been fatally shot and that I had been privileged to serve with him in both the Middle East and the Far East.

"I was also able to give her a photograph of his gravestone in Korea, which she had never seen, because I went back there to revisit the cemetery about 19 years ago and took pictures of all the Leicester Regiment graves. This is the kind of moment that makes my week – and it happens remarkably often!"

On another occasion he was tapped on the shoulder by a man who said: "You probably don't know me, but I know you. You carried me down to the medical tent in Korea after my leg was wounded with bullets, 57 years ago." Two other solders had helped Frank at the time and it was these names that he was asked to find on the Armed Forces Memorial, among the 1,195 people who lost their lives in Korea. "Until then I did not know they were there," Frank says. "I didn't realise they had died in Korea."

While he gets great satisfaction from helping people find the memorials that commemorate a loved one or friend, he finds the Armed Forces Memorial extremely moving.

"My memories don't trouble me at all but I do find it difficult showing people the names on the walls," he says. "It's the blank walls that really get to me, because there is room for more names and I know that more names are going to be added. Those blank walls are the worst place in the Arboretum – that's why it's so hard to go up there."

• • •

Image Credits

Page   6   The Armed Forces Memorial, Courtesy of Ocean Barefoot
Page   8   The Armed Forces Memorial from 'Watersmeet', Courtesy of Ocean Barefoot
Page 10   Private Harry Farr
Page 13   The Shot at Dawn Memorial, Courtesy of Ocean Barefoot
Page 17   In memory of her grandfather, Courtesy of Janet Booth
Page 18   Elaine remembers her lung donor, Courtesy of David Faul
Page 21   Elaine visits the Armed Forces Memorial, Courtesy of David Faul
Page 25   Elaine with statues on the Armed Forces Memorial, Courtesy of David Faul
Page 27   Elaine with the tree dedicated to her lung donor, Courtesy of David Faul
Page 28   Andrew Grundy
Page 31   Sergeant Carl Grundy raising money for the NMA, Courtesy of Carl Grundy
Page 33   Remembered within the Armed Forces Memorial, Courtesy of Ocean Barefoot
Page 35   Sergeant Carl Grundy at the Armed Forces Memorial, Courtesy of Carl Grundy
Page 36   Jenny and Bill Green, Courtesy of Jenny Green
Page 39   The Royal Air Force Association Memorial, Courtesy of Ocean Barefoot
Page 41   Jenny Green at the NMA, Courtesy of Jenny Green
Page 43   Names on the Armed Forces Memorial, Courtesy of Ocean Barefoot
Page 44   Frank Shorter remembers his comrades, Courtesy of the Burton Mail
Page 47   Frank helps young cadets during Armed Forces Week
Page 49   The blank walls of the Armed Forces Memorial, Courtesy of Ocean Barefoot

Acknowledgements

The National Memorial Arboretum wishes to thank Janet Booth,
Elaine Betts, Carl Grundy, Jenny Green and Frank Shorter for their help
in making this book of Life Stories possible. It is stories like theirs that
make the Arboretum the emotional tribute it is today, and underpin
the stunning setting that it will become.

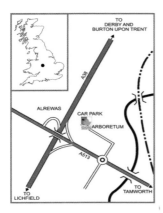

National Memorial Arboretum
Croxall Road
Alrewas
Staffordshire
DE13 7AR

Phone: 01283 792333
Fax: 020 3207 2111

Email: info@thenma.org.uk
Web: www.thenma.org.uk